FEAR OF DOGS & OTHER ANIMALS

FEAR OF DOGS & OTHER ANIMALS

poems

Shauna M. Morgan

CENTRAL SQUARE PRESS

All inquiries and permissions requests should be addressed to the Publisher:

Central Square Press
Lynn, Massachusetts

publisher@centralsquarepress.com
www.centralsquarepress.com

Printed in the United States of America
First Edition

ISBN-13: 978-1-941604-03-8

ISBN-10: 194160403X

Thank you to the editors of the following publications in which these poems first appeared:

Interviewing the Caribbean: "Growing and Weeding" and "Sawdust"; *Pluck! The Journal of Affrilachian Arts & Culture:* "Fear of Dogs and Other Animals"

Cover art: "Amerikkkan Terrorist" © Jason "JaFleu" Fleurant

Book design: Enzo Silon Surin

For those who have been taken, and for we who endure...
especially my brothers Larry, Sheldon, and Andrew

With love to Neena & Ella, my ibejí, and X. Always.

CONTENTS

INTRODUCTION

FEAR OF DOGS & OTHER ANIMALS is a collection for the thirteenth hour, when the day or journey is seemingly half-over and a much needed respite is eminent but is never fully actualized. For those of African descent, the walk home often feels like the day has only just begun.

Shauna M. Morgan, in her debut collection, offers 13 heartrending poems that take us down familiar roads at a time when headlines about advances in race relations contradict the realities of the black experience. In the poem "Riposte XIV", the speaker echoes the sorrow of a familiar cry with the sound indictment "we are not free. we are not safe." These poems should not have been necessary but they are, being both timely and timeless in the way they boldly explore the forgotten spaces some are reluctant to tread.

—Enzo Silon Surin,
Founding Editor & Publisher

fear of dogs & other animals

Perpetual Winter

Even as we march towards spring
there is no letting up.

Children are playing outside,
clomping their feet,
looking to step where it is safe.

Their laughter invites others
and a snowball fight ensues.
Hand grenades of winter
sail between trees, some reaching
their targets, exploding into squeals.

Lights flash across my face,
forcing their way past our curtains.

No one sees the patrol car
until black boots reach the pavement
and hot yellow streams run and mark
the snow at her feet.

Lips now trembling, she looks
towards home, does not know
she must not run.
I never told her not to.

On the insides of my arms,
blue thumbprint bruises
still hold me long afterwards.

The sky, another uniform above us,
a final lesson on dirt and flowers,
and snow.

Needle Work

...I went in search of the secret of what has fed that muzzled and often mutilated, but vibrant, creative spirit that the black woman has inherited, and that pops out in wild and unlikely places to this day.
–Alice Walker *"In Search of Our Mothers' Gardens"*

Before this place,
me and mama and her sisters
would sit around a mound of soft cotton,
patches of every kind,
stitching together our story.

Every woman would sew and tell,
sew and tell her piece until it needled
up with another part of the truth.

In here, we sit in a rectangle of rows,
a room of humming Singers,
the song louder than our voices
without Mary Carter blues.

I prefer it to the night noises
vibrating from this dark block.

Wrapped in plain cloth,
I tug and tear, tug and tear at the seams,
undo the hems into jagged edges
and zig-zag thread, a string of white

coiled around my thumb, a finger spool.

They tell us to make invisible lines,
but everything I see moves like water,
curves into running or whipstitch.

I never made my mark
except on a piece of fabric.

Sometimes, I make a pattern
that trails far beyond this place.

I hum and sing myself
miles away from this square,
sit in a circle of free women,
feel how to shape a story and a life.

Vines

The yard was already overgrown
when we moved in

two-year olds at my knees learning
leaves of three, let it be

the ivy hung and grew
slinking around us

by summer the hydrangea roots
were wrapped away, blue flowers

reaching out to the sun
toward the patch I had cleared

one day in rubber boots
and gloves, clippers in hand

only trimming to the earth
not digging up the poisoned vines

so that the milkweed and dahlia
and lazy susan and lantana

could not be reached after two weeks

except by monarchs and eastern swallowtail

and other creatures that dared to grow
and live and search for nectar

Der Pfau

We hurried past the flower shop
on Portlandstrasse.
There was still light and I clutched
their little fingers,
Meine Zwillinge.
"Mama, *gestorben* means died."

All that time
she had been chasing her peacocks
and scooting around the backyard
under nesberry trees with him,
trying to render loss into locution.
Gestorben means died?

I did not know.
Ich verstehe nicht,
I do not understand
gestorben.

And I do not want this plane
to cross this dark sea,
to land on that soil because
then it will be real.

I do not want to feel

the sharp gravel on my bare feet,
to see the wet grass flashing
blue-green where the proudest bird
has left his feathers.

I do not want this burden,
to collect the plumes
for the vase near his desk,
to lament the years away,
the time not spent,
the silences.

I do not want to know this word
gestorben.

Fear of Dogs and Other Animals

My brother would tell me
not to run from a vicious dog,
not to show fear,
but to greet his teeth
with my own
and even growl.

I didn't know what he knew
about dogs,
except that he could handle
a pit on a chain
better than anyone.
That he hated hounds
and German shepherds
and poodles and collies—
which I called Lassie-dogs
until I was very grown.

My brother would tell me
that white folks love their dogs
more than they like us,
that they would rather their dogs
eat steak and sleep in beds
and on plush sofas
than see us

make a way.

I didn't know what he knew
about white folks,
except that he worked
for a man named Gist
who had a big car
and always had pictures
with the mayor.

Sometimes my brother would
get stopped by the police
after driving that man somewhere.
And sometimes he would get
pocks in his cheeks from bits
of asphalt, and black top stains
on the front of his pants.

My brother used to tell me
to never walk home
on Maple Street,
but to go the long way
down King,
and always with my friends.

I didn't know what he knew
about Maple,

except that he said there
were dogs and men
who could tear into flesh,
that canine teeth and hot bullets
were never shy or hesitant,
that white folks know
dogs and guns like
we know death and poverty.

He knew.
Except he knew too well.

Résumé Names

We gave them white résumé names.
I had a different list and lingered
on every letter, enunciating and singing
each syllable, whispering at first then
shouting them, laughing them out
feeling the way they vibrated on my tongue
and blew from my lips.

Then I read each meaning,
searched for a root, something free
anchored only by legacy and heritage.
Black and brown names scented
by bissap and masala, flavors to anoint
tiny feet and wrinkled heads of dark hair,
bundles wrapped in batik and kanga,
mouths rooting at my breasts.

I wanted names as dark as my areolae
and the insides of my mother's thighs,
strong as an umbilical tug, sharp
as the contractions that drew them out,
determined as my will, more unyielding,
even, than his last word.

Renewal

We left the flowers in the car
—too much rain.

I stood there holding mama's umbrella.
She looked up to the sky, as if asking

God, when dis a guh done?

Rainfall filled up the rectangular hole,
and we backed away as the sides caved
in little pieces at a time.

I stood where his feet should be,
my toes squeezing the mud
that filled my new shoes and socks—

watching as the work-men were
knee-deep and bailing water.

The earth was refusing his body.

We backed away again,
stamping the wet loamy soil,
watching the earth say no, too.

Sawdust

The lumber stretches long and hard,
pocked like your legs,
a home for sores round and brown,
a center-crust of yellow,
a community of imperfections.

I inhale.

It is your smell, without you.
Without your sweat and the metallic
odor on top of wood.
Without flecks of sawdust in your
silver-at-night hair.

I inhale you.
A sanitized, pre-treated, uncut,
unbolted, unhinged you—
your smell in the morning,
six o' clock punch,
sawdust shavings under your feet,
Coleman in your hand,
ice-cold *bickle* in this land for me,
triangle trusses on your back for me.

A chip off the old block,

or rather curled and curled shavings,
delicate but unfeminine—
"you are just like your father."
Heavy feet, bones marching,
steel toes hammering the ground.
And your smell,
no longer mahogany.
Pine. Cypress.

We went to buy plywood
but got Birch instead.
The storm would have taken
our roof and left the windows intact.
We would have blown out like these
shavings, golden fibers in a whirling
cyclone, inhaled and lodged in the lungs.

I inhale you.

Growing and Weeding

I've always lived in the midst of things that grew
faster than I: My mother's white roses,
our coolie-plum tree, my cousin Charmaine,
whose breasts appeared overnight, and sent me
to the bathroom pressing my arms against my chest.

I tried to grow things too: a young chicken
fallen from the Caribbean Broilers truck,
my sister's cherry tree, thyme in the Virginia
winter, a Jade plant from the Baxter brothers
who were not brothers at all, a white Dendrobium
that flowered once.

When I wondered why things tended to die, he said
it was me, that I killed everything green, especially money.

But today I remembered how I grew things, how I cared
for African violets, never letting water touch the velvet
leaves, how the purple flowers would burst and burst.
I birthed children, two at once, and grew them
in a garden of heirloom tomatoes and yellow gladioli.

Today, I will plant raspberry bushes for summer,
and soon dahlias, giant sunflowers, and moonshine
yarrow for the vase in our kitchen.

The children and I will harvest Black Krim and zucchini,
pick gungo peas and cut ripe honeydew from our new vines,
weeding as we go.

Live Oak

My roots run deep,
down into this soil
watered by the salt-spray borne
by my foremothers,
on whose limbs little white boys
climbed and hung their swings.

These heavy boughs,
thick and ligneous, spreading wide
and low enough for a man
to lean, rest his back
and hide behind the curtain
of Spanish moss soft enough
for the wind to murmur,
tell truths that come quietly
sometimes in wispy hushes.

His heritage runs deep too,
bloody tap-root, a bourbon barrel
ablaze, a beam in a dark cabin,
a boy-child without a likeness,
a resurrection fern,
fronds wrapped and waiting.

(Re)Kindling

1.
He found me, not quite asleep,
in the hollow of a thicket
on a bed of lightwood.
And I, no longer green,
would have burst into flames
at the sight of him,
at the sound of his voice,
if not for the river and the moon
and the steady hand of the universe.

2.
When I stood and stepped out
holding his scarred arm,
I felt the acute sensation of his touch
move me to intoxication,
a fervid vertigo
spinning me into the sunset
and into the darkness that followed.

3.
It was there he set me ablaze
with word and touch and gifts
unexplained by time.
And when he heaped onto me

all the weight of oak
and a fire as ancient as the sun,
I ignited, became new.

4.
I imagine him now,
having left me seared
in my newness,
kindling old fires sacred as the wind,
moving slowly to remember
precisely how he yearned to a flash,
how he rendered a life into embers
beautiful and warm,
the remains of something familiar.

Blood

She looked away,
not wanting to see the yellow paleness,
soft wrinkled face thrust to her breast
before she even began to push away
the sack and the weight of blood and life
still in her.

He took to it right away
like none of her children before,
sucking steadily, draining her
into a kind of sleep and exhaustion,
little milky baby
who heard her songs,
knew her voice.

Little misbegotten child.

And she held him there,
feeling the contractions as she pushed again,
expelling all of that red-blue, blue blood,
all that gave life and sustained him.

Riposte XIV: *The* [new] *administration of justice and description of the laws*

after Thomas Jefferson's *Notes on the State of Virginia*

I do not smile, behave, show fear, or shake.
I do not keep my hands on the wheel or look straight ahead.
I let them wait   for   my   answer.
        Do you know how fast you were going?
I put my arm on the door, cock my elbow and point it in their direction.
They will kill me anyway.
I set my gaze to theirs, one pale face at a time.
I wait.
Yes.

If any free person commit an offence against the commonwealth,
if it be below the degree of felony,
he is bound by a justice to appear before their court,
to answer it on indictment or information.

They will kill us anyway.
We are not free.

I do not conjure up tears.
I do not loosen the top buttons on my blouse.
I do not stay in my seat,
or call them sir or ma'am.
I do not explain.

My wallet is in the trunk.
I do not get back in the car.
I do not submit to their bullshit request.

Let's see what else you have in the trunk?
I stand with arms folded.
I let them wait for my answer.

No.
They will kill me anyway.

If the criminal be a slave
the trial by [~~the county court~~ any armed, near-white person]
is final.

I do not move. I do not unfold my arms.
I do not look away.
I do not change my answer.
I do not let my pounding heart move me to a tremble.
I do not cry.
I do not look in the direction of two new flashing lights.
Which one will be the killer today?

We are not free.
We are not safe.
They will kill us anyway.

Notes

1. The Mary Carter referenced in "Needle Work" was impris-oned at Mississippi State Penitentiary, also known as Parch-man Farm, and was well known for her blues songs—all of which were recorded while she was imprisoned.

2. German words in "Der Pfau"

> *Der Pfau:* The peacock
> *Meine Zwillinge*: My twins
> *Gestorben:* Died
> *Ich verstehe nicht*: I do not understand

3. Cultural references in "Résumé Names"

Bissap: The national beverage of Senegal, bissap is brewed from the *Hibiscus sabdariffa,* also commonly known as sorrel in Jamaica and much of the Caribbean.

Masala: The Hindi word for spice, masala can be made of sev-eral combinations of ground herbs and spices.

Batik: Originating in Indonesia, batik is a technique of decorat-ing cloth using wax and dye. Valued across the world, batiks have even been found wrapped on Egyptian mummies. This method has been widely used across much of West Africa since the mid-nineteenth century, and hand-crafted batiks are often made with patterns and symbols representing distinct ethnic groups in Ghana and Nigeria, for example.

Kanga: These full body-length colorful cotton cloths emerged on the horn of Africa and are commonly worn in places like Burundi, the Democratic Republic of Congo, Kenya, Rwanda, Tanzania and Uganda.

4. The line *"God, when dis a guh done?"* is Jamaican Patois and can be loosely translated as "God, when will this be finished?"

5. In "Sawdust" bickle is a Jamaican Patois word meaning food, usually warmed items brought from home.

6. The second and fifth stanzas of "Riposte XIV" are taken from Thomas Jefferson's *Notes on the State of Virginia.*

about the author

A poet and scholar, **Shauna M. Morgan** springs from a rural district in Clarendon, Jamaica and holds an enduring love for the Diaspora about which she writes. She has published scholarly works in *Bulletin of the School of Oriental and African Studies, Journal of Postcolonial Writing*, and *South Atlantic Review*. Her poetry has appeared in *ProudFlesh: New Afrikan Journal of Culture, Politics & Consciousness, The Pierian, Pluck! The Journal of Affrilachian Arts & Culture, Anthology of Appalachian Writers Volume VI, Interviewing the Caribbean* and elsewhere. Morgan researches and teaches literature of Africa and the African Diaspora at Howard University in Washington, D.C., and she lives in Virginia with her twin daughters.